'Tis As It Was

ISBN 978-1-4466-4206-1

Per
Filius
Publishing

'Tis As It Was

A Memoir with Poetry

Norrie O'Mahony

*I dedicate this book with love and affection to Nannie my much loved Aunt
who gave me such a happy childhood, wonderful memories
and a love of reading and books.*

My favourite inspirational quotation is from the great German writer Goethe;

"Whatever you can do or dream you can, begin it, boldness has genius, power and magic in it, begin it now."

So here goes…

For a long time I have been thinking of writing a book with some poems included, as you read this book I hope it will bring you joy, laughter and happy memories.

My first home was converted waiting rooms previously used by Lord Bandon to wait for the passing train, this house was at the end of a long avenue to Castle Bernard. My father was a railway man and I lived there with my parents, brothers and sisters. The house comprised of hallway, a large kitchen with a Stanley Range for heating and cooking, a passage with two bedrooms, one very big with fireplace, and a toilet and cellar. As one came in from the road you could go through a gateway or over a wall with a style. Then you walked a short distance and crossed over the railway line. On your left then was a gate at the entrance to the house, over which grew a bough of pink roses, and a pathway with a wooden fence outside of which was a platform and the railway track. As the train passed one could see the people in the carriages. Around the back of the house some steps led down to a small garden in which grew some blackcurrant and gooseberry bushes, a small apple tree and lots of that lovely creeping plant, Our Lady's Carpet, with its little white flowers, all these were there since Lord Bandon's time.

On Sundays in the summertime many people would go for a walk through the castle grounds. Along the avenue there were some lovely shrubs and a lake still had a lot of water-lilies on it. Just the ruins of the once stately castle remain as it was burnt down the time of the Troubles. The entrance was still in good condition and one could go down into the wine cellars and inside could be seen where the big fireplaces used to be, and here too the echoes and memories remain. You could walk right through the grounds out on the road opposite to the town park with its little wooden bridge over the river and acres carpeted with bluebells. This place too has its history as some young men were shot and left there by the Black and Tans during the Trouble times. Iron crosses mark where they fell and their names on them and the date.

The following is a poem I wrote about peace in Ireland.

Peace In Ireland

Peace be with you in abundance,
Coming from our God on high.
Ever lasting in its goodness,
Bringing happiness and joy.
In this emerald isle of Ireland
Let all war and hatred cease.
Come extend the hand of friendship,
Let us smoke the pipe of peace.
In this war there is no honour,
It's a feud begot of hate,
When we plan to kill our neighbour
For he is of different faith.
If we follow in Gods footsteps,
O'er our land His grace will flow,
It will melt away all evil,
As the sunshine does the snow.
Time in passing changes all things,
All on Earth in time will cease.
Happy he who in his wisdom,
Listens to the Prince of Peace.

One day my Mam was brushing the hall and the front door was opened. She heard a rustling sound and a lady wearing a long black dress minus her head passed through the hall and down the stone steps to the cellar. Feeling very shocked she leant against the wall stunned at what she had seen, or was her mind playing tricks?, when my six year old sister who was playing outside in the pathway ran in and said, "Mam, who is the lady that came in without a head?". On another occasion my parents saw a tall fair haired young man coming up the path and into the hall, but when they opened the kitchen door there was no one there. The covers on the kitchen range were often lifted and replaced noisily at night.

Nearby was the little village of Old Chapel. This village was very self sufficient, it consisted of a small public house owned by a midwife and her sister, a man who made coffins, a dairy, a mill, a forge and a shop owned by a lady called Maggie. I have fond memories of Maggie's shop especially of how it looked at Christmas time. Christmas when you are young is magical and so was Maggie's window.

Maggie's Window

Though many years have now gone by,
More than I'd care remember,
My thoughts roll back to childhood days
And Maggie's Christmas window.
Her little shop so neat and bright,
At Christmas was a child's delight.
She kept tea and sugar, bread and buns,
And Sunlight Soap that would last for months.
With jars of sweets in a colourful row
Liquorice pipes with a fiery glow.
Sugar-of-candy that hung on a string
And all kinds of biscuits she kept in a tin.
She sold Santa's with a wick beneath,
I got one as a special treat.
When the wick was lit, out toys would pop.
Oh! The wonderful things in Maggie's Shop.

As a little one with my brother I stood
Outside her window at Christmas time.
In my minds eye I can see it still.
The toys and dolls and the shining star over the manger,
And we looked in awe at the Baby Jesus
On His bed of straw.
And the Santa face so plump and bright,
It filled my dreams that Christmas night.
Her nieces from the U.S.A.
Helped Maggie make that grand display.
Great stores I've seen since that Christmas time
With toys and music and lights sublime,
But with Maggie's shop they don't compare.
Somehow the spirit of Christmas was captured there.

I remember being very upset shortly before one Christmas, my brother who was eight years older than me came running in to the house and gave me a piece of holly saying it was off Santa's hat and that Santa had been killed by the last train that passed. I finally stopped crying when my mother coming in said Santa couldn't be killed as he was an Angel and that he would be coming for sure on Christmas Eve.

The forge was worked by two brothers, Dell and Jack. One wet day part of the gable-end of their house collapsed, a passer-by said,

"God Dell what happened your house!"

"Yera nothing!" said Dell, "We just got the light and water in the same day."

If they had a fight Dell wouldn't give Jack any breakfast and would have to go to a friends house instead. Not wanting to go with his hands hanging he'd pick some groundsel (a little wild plant that's a favourite of birds) from the hedgerow for his friends caged bird. One time a farmer asked him what was he picking and he said he was picking flowers because Dell wouldn't have his breakfast unless there was flowers on the table!

While we were there a railway worker called Paddy lodged with us, he was quite a character and did not mind sleeping in the cellar. A little bit up the line from our house there was a shanty, which was a small shed with a stove, table and seats. These shantys were here and there along the line so the railway workers could have shelter and eat their lunch on wet days. Sometimes my father and a few of the men would go there at night to play cards. On not being invited to join after a few turns, Paddy took action. He managed to put a piece of slate on top of the pipe coming from the stove and smoked them out!

If anyone came in who could not stay long, or was in a hurry Paddy would tell them to sit down if they only stayed a week!

Another one of his sayings was birds of identical plumage invariably congregate in close proximity.

The yearly mission was much looked forward to, a week for the women and a week for the men. One evening my Mam said to Paddy that he was going very early.

"I have to!" replied Paddy,

"Last night I was standing at the back of the church when that disappointed Jesuit marched me up to the top of the middle aisle to get me a seat".

He was referring to a man who had left the Seminary but was still very involved in the church. He would also entertain the people passing in the train by walking around on a pair of stilts that he had made himself.

Once the train, nearly having run out of fuel, stopped and got some old sleepers that were at the side of our house from my Mam, enough to get them to the station a mile or so away. While they were getting them ready to put them into the engine a woman came in and asked to have a bottle heated for her baby. Mam used to say there was a touch of '*Are you right there Michael*', Percy French's song, about it.

Across the road from us was a high gateway, and a long tree lined avenue leading to a big house in which lived a lady called Mrs. Sherlock. She employed a gardener called Tim. On wet days Tim always wore a coat covered by a cape and two hats.

She would look out and say,

"Here comes Connolly with his entire wardrobe!".

When she was not well my aunt and another lady were employed to look after her. One day my Mam went to have a word with my aunt and she took me with her. I was about four years old at the time. Mrs. Sherlock came to the door, she wore a long dress with black velvet ribbon around her neck and a cameo broach. Her white hair was rolled up. She asked if I liked tea and gave me a present of a small teapot. She was very fond of animals; in her younger days she kept horses and had two small dogs she taught lots of tricks to. She made sure the birds were fed everyday even when she was ill.

The night she died, my brother of about 18 was sent to tell a friend of hers, as he left the house the sound of horses hooves accompanied him down the avenue and joined him again on his way back. He was not frightened, he felt it was some relative of hers who wished to keep him company.

Those who worked on the railway on the whole were a very special lot of people always in good form and the picturesque country stations had an atmosphere all their own with their neat flower beds and cosy waiting rooms. It was a great pity when the GSR (Great Southern Railway) closed. It was so nice and relaxing travelling in the old steam trains with their cheerful whistle.

I remember lying in bed one New Year's eve and hearing the driver of the mail train blowing the whistle at midnight until he reached the nearby station.

An elderly man my father knew, as his son worked on the railway, on hearing that my father was going on holiday to England asked if he could travel with him as he wished to visit a son over there and could not manage the journey alone. Those who worked on the station decided they would give them a good send off. They arranged with the engine driver and put some detonators on the rails to go off for some distance after the train left the station. The old man who was noted for his colourful language, after the initial shock left a swear out of him to say what he would do to the so and so's on that so and so station when he got back.

When I was about seven, my father was transferred to Drimoleague as inspector. One evening a goat arrived on the goods train and was taken off to resume its journey the next day. The station masters daughter was playing around and took the label saying its final destination off its horn and tied it to her leg. After spending some time running and jumping around the station, she lost it. This left the poor animal stranded until they later found out where it was going. In the meantime it was well looked after by the station masters wife. I think it says a lot about a person if they are kind to animals, they return it so much and we can learn a lot from them. To be at one with animals and nature is a wonderful gift. St Francis referred to animals as his brothers and sisters. As the great man of peace Gandhi once said,

'The greatness of a nation and its moral progress can be judged by the way its animals are treated'.

The following is a little poem I wrote about animals, nature and love.

We Thank Thee Lord

We thank thee Lord for everything,
For little birds upon the wing.
For busy bees and butterflies,
Sunny days and bright blue skies.
For animals and cuddly things,
For all the joy each season brings.
For snow and wind and things that grow,
Help us Dear Lord good seeds to sow.
For babbling streams and rivers wide,
For mountains high and green hillside.
For waves that break upon the shore.
For these we thank Thee Lord and more.
For home and love and Your guiding light,
Like the shining moon in the darkening night.

We lived in a rented bungalow, in the next house there was a family of eight children, so we had lots of company. Just one field separated us from a farm house in which lived a widow woman and her son. He would visit us most nights and was nice company. An uncle of his lived in Drinagh and he would come to help him at time of threshing and cutting turf for the winter. We soon got to know this Uncle Johnny, and looked forward to his visits as much as they did. He would come in the door take off his cap and say God bless all here, he would sit by the fire and after a chat with my parents, ask us were we ready for a story. Sometimes he'd start off and say,

"I have a good story for ye tonight...right yera man here we are."

He was a real seanchai. It was nearly always ghost-stories and he would assure us every word of it was true. There was one about the night he met Jackie the lantern, a ghost who would not let you get home. Johnny knew the fields like the back of his hand but could not find his way until he sat down and turned his coat inside out. Only then did he make headway for home. That was fine until it was our bedtime. At that time houses were lit with oil-lamps and candles. The top of our front door was of different colour glass. When the lamp was lit it cast an eerie glow over the long hallway. We would dash across the hall to our bedroom with the thoughts of Johnny's apparitions with chains giving us extra speed.

My Mam would always have something special with his cup of tea on his last night. Johnny would say,

"God bless your flowery heart!"

We said goodbye to Johnny and looked forward to seeing him again. I can still remember one of his sayings that if you had your health, peace, love and the grace of God, you had more than money could buy.

The Robin

A little bit of Heaven came to visit me today.
It hopped around the garden,
In its fascinating way.
It ate the food I placed for it
And sang a cheerful song,
This feisty little robin,
How I wished that it would stay.
But it left a simple message,
As it gaily flew away,
It's the little things in life that count.
They bring us the most joy.
And happiness comes from within,
It's something you cannot buy.

Every year we went to my Gran's house in Bandon for Christmas, she lived there with her daughter who was my favourite Aunt. I was always asking to be left stay with her. We went on the morning train, a day or so before Christmas Eve, and our dog Huggins a little terrier came with us. She always took a window seat so she could look out! Christmas, at that time began just a few weeks before in the shops, and each shop gave their customers something extra in their basket when they did their Christmas shopping, such as a cake or special candle. The *Hollybough* and *Ireland's Own* were two Christmas issues everyone looked forward to, they can still be got today. We always got Curley-Wee and Rupert Christmas annuals. To my Gran the Christmas candle was very important, she would have it dressed up in red or white crepe paper depending on the colour of the candle with some holly on the top. This would be lit on Christmas Eve, she being the oldest would sprinkle the holy-water on it and I being the youngest got to light it. When it was lit she would say, "Go meimid beo ar an tam seo aris." (May we be alive this time again)

My uncle and his wife who lived down the town always called on Christmas Eve, after the ceremony of the candle the men would have a drink and the women make the tea and Christmas cake. We would have lemonade, something you got during the year only if you were sick. My Gran would have, as she said herself, a drop of punch. We were up early for mass on Christmas morning after which we went to see the crib at the end of the church and then home to breakfast.

After a big dinner (the highlight of which to us children was that luscious Christmas pudding, which had been hanging from the kitchen ceiling for the previous few weeks to mature) we would then sit in the room by the cosy fire, and read. One year we got that wonderful girls story; *Little Women* and another year *Alice in Wonderland.*

Around this time we moved from the bungalow to a house a little further down the road, again we were very near the railway line, opposite us was a house in which a girl from Whiddy Island worked. She came to visit us most nights and she was good fun. One very hot day she saw a couple of the men she knew working on the line opposite, she cut up some oranges on a plate and took them over to them - having first sprinkled each piece with salt! They were delighted and thanked her so much. My mother on hearing a lot of screeching ran out and was surprised to see Margaret sitting on the grass verge by the railway line while the railway men rubbed her face with the pieces of orange. Her face was red and sore for a few days, they said she got off light with a free beauty treatment.

In those days People got together more and made their own entertainment and fun, most people owned a radio which was battery operated. My brother had a gramophone with a selection of records, which was often borrowed for birthday parties or if the girls in the local post office were having some celebration or other. One or two of the railway men would come some nights to play cards with my father and brother, they would usually have some tea and biscuits or whatever. One evening my sister and I thought we would have some fun, seeing some Kerry Cream biscuits in the press we took them up to our room and spent quite some time taking out the cream coloured filling and putting in a thin slice of soap. That night when my Mam made the tea we helped putting the biscuits on a plate, we watched with glee the expressions on the railway mens faces. The poor men were too polite to say anything, until we saw some soap suds coming through my fathers' false teeth. We made a hasty retreat to our bedroom. Lucky for us my father, who would now be known as having a short fuse, had calmed down by the time he had washed his teeth. We got off with a lecture and were told we had gone down a hundred feet in his estimation.

A mile or so out the road from us lived an old lady and her son who was a shoemaker, he was always busy and his favourite saying was-

God send the rain and real bad weather to lift the sole from the upper leather.

They had a nice little house with a field at the side of it where she kept her donkey. She would pass our place every Friday in her donkey and cart going to the village to collect her pension and do some shopping. The donkey would be going full speed on his way down, she could hardly stay sitting in the cart. He was in a hurry for the weekly treat she gave him of a bun and a bottle of Guinness, which the publican poured into a bowl she brought. On the way home he took his time and we would often hear her as they passed saying,

'Go on Neddy, hurry up!' - With little results.

All this time I had been asking to go back to Bandon to live with my aunt. My parent's eventually agreed and I was delighted. I always had a special bond with my aunt who some years before had lost her three children through illnesses and her husband shortly after in an accident. I was very happy going to the convent school there. I went back home for the school holidays so had the best of both worlds. It was nice too, to meet up with the friends from the Drimoleague School, not that I had many happy memories of being there! The uniform consisted of a white apron and many of the children came in their bare feet even in winter time. The teachers were not very nice and used the cane a lot, their teaching left an awful lot to be desired. I remember well trying to read and understand my Irish book at home one evening, having been just told to learn the next page, I kept asking my mother to help me. I may as well have been asking how to get to the moon as she did not know any Irish, how I dreaded going to school the next day knowing I would get slapped! On another occasion not having opened my book quick enough at reading time the teacher, still standing at her desk, used her long bamboo cane and hit me on my wrist. It swelled up and she had to run the cold tap in the hall on it for some time. One of the local Garda came up one day very cross as his daughters legs were cut by the use of a bamboo cane.

The map of Ireland hung just inside the door of the classroom at the back of the school, a girl from the village was given a pointer to point out where county Donegal was. In her haste, probably due to her joy that she knew the answer, she tore the map. We felt so sorry for her all the slaps she got. The boys were in a separate part of the school and they were treated worse than us. A local Doctor sent his sons, after a court case, to the Protestant school and another man from the village gave the teacher what she had given his son after the boy went home having been beaten by her.

After some years Margaret, the girl who worked in the house across from us decided she was going to England, when she came to say goodbye on her last evening she asked my mother to put on her favourite record – *When You and I Were Young Maggie*. We were all sad to see her go and missed her a lot. A year or so later she wrote to my Mam to say she was coming on holidays and that she would be on the evening train on such a date going home to Whiddy Island and to have my Mam be in the garden as the train passed and she would throw out a present she had for her. It landed safely amid much waving.

Shamrock & Clover

Take me back where the shamrock is growing
And I'll be in clover once more,
Take me back where the shamrock is growing
And I'll be in clover once more.
Take me back where the land is the greenest,
Where the streamlets like silver they flow,
Let me lie 'neath the gorse on the heather,
It's the nearest to Heaven I know.
Let me walk through her fields in the Springtime,
Let me stroll through her woodlands in Fall,
Let me sit by her firesides in Winter,
And the Seanachai stories recall.
Take me back where the peat fires are burning,
Where the stranger is welcome as kin,
Where there's always a céad mile failte,
And that someone to welcome you in.
Let us keep all our Irish traditions,
In this land that St. Patrick once trod.
It was not just the luck of the Irish,
T'was they honoured their Maker and God.

We had cooking class once a week with one of the nuns, so one Christmas time I decided to make a Christmas cake at home. The recipe said to soak the fruit over-night in whiskey or brandy. I put some on the fruit as instructed and the pub being only two doors away I got some extra and put some in the cake mixture the following day as well. It was rather late when I put it in the oven so we decided to stay up until it was cooked. After some hours we heard a loud bang. On looking there was a big hole in the middle of the cake! It had exploded due to all the spirits I had put in. My aunt said we had our own private volcano. We finished the cooking of it hoping for the best, it smelt very nice anyway. An old gentleman who lived near us who was partial to fruitcake had some of it and survived. I always remember my friend bending over laughing looking at it and my aunt telling her we had our breakfast before going to bed.

It was a long walk to the Convent school in Bandon, the school was on top of a high hill above the town. From our side pupils had to walk New road, Market street, Begleys lane, over the foot bridge and then up Kilbrogan and Convent hill. Begleys had a lot of toys in the many windows along the lane way where they had a paper shop. The following few lines applied to us children going that way.

Along Begleys Lane we went to school,

We would drop in on the way

To see Mr Begley give the paper

To the Dog that called each day.

There we got our pencils and our rubbers

Our copybooks and pens.

And we'd loiter at those windows

Going to school and back again.

I enjoyed visiting my uncle and his wife who lived nearer the town, she always invited me to tea and pancakes with them on Shrove Tuesday. She would call in to see us a few evenings a week when she went for a walk. One particular evening she came wearing a nice cream coloured coat her daughter had sent her from Scotland. We saw her off as usual at the door, it was when she walked away we saw the big black circle at the back of her coat. My aunt was in a state as it was then she remembered resting the pot she had been boiling clothes in on the chair she had sat on. On her next visit she said she was as upset about how many people had seen her that evening as she was about the coat, anyway she had managed to get it cleaned, and after a while we had a good laugh about it.

As well as their daughter who was married in Scotland they had a son who went to work in England, he kept in contact at first but sadly seven years went by during which they did not hear from him. They were very worried not knowing what had happened to him. One evening she called to us as usual and she said to my Aunt,
"As you know I have been praying all those years for news of Jerry to St. Jude, well last night I put the prayer

leaflet away and said Saint Jude I've been praying to you all these years and you have not answered me so I won't ask for your help any more."

 A few days later they came to tell us that they had received a telegram from their daughter to say Jerry would be coming home shortly! They were so delighted. They later heard the full story. The daughter had been in London with a friend and saw Jerry standing at a bus stop. She said at first she could hardly believe it was him, it was a chance in a million to find him. He went to stay with her a while and then came home. He later worked in Cork and married there so there was a happy ending. She was very grateful to Saint Jude who answered her after all.

One day on her way up to the church to pay a visit, she met a woman with a little girl on the church hill. They got talking and the woman told her she was going specially with her little daughter to the grotto at the end of the church to thank Our Lady for answering her prayers. She had been going to the Grotto for some weeks asking for help to get the clothes for her little girls Holy Communion. And the previous day on her way down from the church she met a woman she knew who asked her if she knew anyone who would like communion clothes as she had them all belonging to her daughter from the previous year. Now she was so grateful, she said she had collected them and that they were just perfect. I think this is a wonderful example of what faith in prayer can achieve.

In the street in Bandon where we lived there were only five houses and a Bar so we were very close, the neighbours were more like relations, everyone helped each other. Opposite was a river a lawn and trees, it was only a short walk to the town. I remember one time when a neighbour called to ask my aunt to go over to the river wall to persuade her husband to come out of the river or he'd get pneumonia. We knew he'd been in bed with flu. He had been eating an orange and put the peelings on the bedside table where he had also put his false teeth. She had cleared away the orange peel and threw it with some rubbish in the river, not noticing the false teeth. Now he was in the river looking for them. Sadly he never found his teeth. It was later they had a good laugh about it.

A young man who lived further down the road, one evening was cutting overhanging branches on one of the trees opposite. He was sitting on a branch over the river cutting the ones near him, someone passing on the footpath went over talking to him and being distracted with the talk he cut the branch he was sitting on and fell into the river. Luckily he was not hurt and those who helped him out could not but laugh seeing the funny side of it.

One summer being at home on holidays from my first job in Bandon for two weeks, one of my brothers on holidays also asked me to help him with some turf he had cut in a bog between Drimoleague and Skibbereen. At first I was undecided as it sounded like very hard work, but eventually said I would give it a go. We left early each morning and cycled the few miles to the bog, taking with us a Primus stove, sandwiches and all the things we needed to make tea. As we cycled along that first morning I could not help but notice all the spiders' webs shining with the morning dew like fragile decorations on the hedgerows. Though like many others I am not a lover of spiders I had to give them credit for such perfect workmanship and design. When we arrived at the bog he already had some turf cut and dried in small stooks which we put into a panger and taking a handle each took up to a ditch near the road and stacked it ready for the lorry. After a few hours it was time for something to eat. There was a spring well nearby and we sure enjoyed the refreshing tea and sandwiches. It's true to say hunger is the best sauce. I was surprised how much I enjoyed that week, in spite of all the creepy crawlies-the likes of some I had never seen before including centipedes and small lizards. There were some lovely unusual flowers growing there in wonderful shades of purple,red and pink and bog cotton on it's green stalk moving like bits of cotton wool in the breeze, said to have got there from a leprechauns beard as he danced around with his crock of gold at May Eve, a special time in fairyland.

My week in the open air had given me a terrific tan so when I got back to work they would not believe me when I told them about my stint in the bog, and said I must have been using some tanning lotion!

Seasons

Spring is here, this Lady grand,
Spreads her mantle o'er the land.
Waking up the seedlings there,
Soon they're peeping everywhere.
Birds are busy building nests,
All around there's bustle and zest.
All is wonderful, it's true,
Everything must start anew.
Birds and bees and butterflies,
Fly enchanted through the skies.
Babies sleeping in their cots,
Wondrous times of tiny tots.

Then comes Summer's happy days,
All in life is young and gay.
Children laughing, having fun,
Basking in the noonday sun.
School days, college, husband, wife,
Building homesteads full of life.
Loving, being loved, in a haze,
Happy hours and work filled days.

But 'Old Time' keeps moving on,
All too soon our Summers gone.
Autumn song creeps o'er the plane,
All the land must sleep again.

Autumn is come for all to see,
The leaves are falling from each tree.
It's time for the squirrels, their nuts to store,
Time for the little moles to bore
Into the earth, so warm and brown,
Soon they will snuggle softly down.
Time for little girls and boys,
To put away their summer toys.
It's time for change, a letting go,
Serenity and going slow.
A sense of joy in work well done,
Like Autumn colours, a richness spun.

Soon the Winter winds will blow,
Nothing then, but cold and snow.
Blazing fires and cosy chats,
Rocking chairs and granny flats.
Every season brings its good,
As the Lord ordained it should.
Winter brings us Christmas joy,
With toys for every girl and boy.
And the hope, a future lies,
Far away, beyond the skies.
Bought for you and bought for me,
By Our Saviour on a tree.

We were not long living in Drimoleague when my Mam noticed a very pretty young girl dressed in a grey coat shopping in the village. She enquired from a shopkeeper as to who she was and was told she was the youngest of a large family who lived in a cottage on a farm owned by a business man in the village. She lived there with her parents and a sister who did dressmaking. A few of her siblings were in different counties in Ireland and the rest had emigrated to England and the U.S. Her sister did some sewing for us on a few occasions. Their white cottage with its nice garden and long open fire place always looked so neat and homely. Her mother was a very remarkable woman. She minded two children for someone in the village and took in washing which she managed to do by getting water from a stream nearby and the clothes, when washed, she rinsed there. All this extra work to make ends meet. After a few years when the house next to where we lived was for sale the family got together and bought it. My Mam said it was wonderful to see them at work, two or three coming home at a time getting it ready and finally finishing it and putting up curtains. They brought the parents to see it pretending they were just looking at it, she remarked wasn't it grand to have the water in. They then took them down to the room where they had a party laid out and told them it was theirs. They came to live there shortly after. They were a lovely family, so good looking and caring. One summer when I was at home the youngest girl who was on her holidays from England came on the day she was going back and asked if I would stay a while with her Mam after she left on the morning bus. Her Dad had passed away the year before and her Mam would be lonely. When I went in she showed me all the food and treats her daughter had left her. We had a cup of tea and a chat and her daughter who was working in the village came to see her later. My Mam and the other neighbours visited her often. Her grandchildren came during the school holidays. She enjoyed many happy years in her new house.

During this time a new church was built in Drimoleague and an artist from Austria was commissioned to paint the back of the Altar. Different locals posed for him and the people of the village insisted she was one of the first. She can be seen there dressed in her black cloak. It's called All-Saints church. One wintery morning she went to enquire about a neighbour, who was in bed with flu. Sadly, while talking to his wife she got very ill. They got the Doctor for her and contacted her family. I was at home the weekend one of her daughters came to ask my Mam to join them as they were all upstairs with her now and would like her to be there. I went also. She was the first person I was with who was dying. She just went to sleep. They were all truly wonderful to her and said they could never forget all she had done for them.

After she passed away, or as Mam always said went home, many people had some stories praising her. The local tailor told how she made sure her husband had a good suit to wear going to Mass. The midwife who attended the birth of one of the children told how she went back home to get some tea to give her after the baby was born. When she returned the baby was lying beside her, the rest of the children around the bed, and she sitting up mixing a cake for them to put on the bestiple on the fire.

After a few years the farm was for sale where their cottage was. My father bought the farm and after some time one of Mrs. Driscolls sons, Jerry, came on holidays to his sister in the village. One day he called up and asked my Mam if he could go into the cottage to take some photos. She gave him the key and when he came back they had tea and a chat and my brother drove him back to the village. No doubt he was lonely at a time like that, and they were glad to help him.

Mother

Endless feeds and sleepless nights,
The thought just makes me shudder.
All the going day and night;
Who would be a mother?

Happy laughter, baby talk,
Trust that is like no other.
The innocence and love in a baby's smile;
Who would not be a mother!

Having finished my education at the convent I did a secretarial course and then started work as secretary in a local garage, it was a big concern and had a lot employed including eight salesmen, it also did self-drive. All the staff were very pleasant to work with, among them was a young lad who was slightly retarded. We always made sure to be specially nice to him and help him when we could, his name was Peter. I worked there for a good few years and then went to work in Cork.

Having worked in Cork for some time I had a fall and was in plaster for a few months. I could not get out very much. A woman who lived nearby with a niece and nephew always made me welcome. Her niece who was one of my best friends would collect me to watch TV with them at night and there was always tea and some of her wonderful baking. Their kindness meant so much to me at that time. Over the years we have always kept in touch. Her house always looked so cosy and inviting. She could have made a fortune as an interior designer.

Many years passed before I met Peter again in a local restaurant, we had a chat he told me he had Parkinson's disease and I was glad to see him. Some time later I went to work in Bantry for Germans who had started a shoe factory. It was down by the Bay where the old train station was and the station masters house I had previously visited, as my father used to come there, was now used partly as a lodging place and store for the factory. When I answered their advertisement for a secretary I did not come for the arranged interview. I was shopping in Bantry the following week when I mentioned to two men I knew in a shop about the factory and how I had not come for the interview. One of them said why don't you go there now and see how it goes if you are still interested. So I did. Mr Frick, the owner was in his office with a French lady who supervised the sewing department. I nervously introduced myself and apologised for not coming the previous week, he laughed and said – oh you are Irish that is why you are here a week late. He said to come back the following Monday for an interview with a business man he knew in the town as he said his English was not good enough. A manager in a local firm interviewed me, called out some letters which I typed, and told Mr Frick they were OK. Mr Frick said I could start the following week and would be paid end of week only if my work was satisfactory. In many ways I believe things in life are meant to be, as others had been interviewed during that week yet the job seemed to be waiting for me. I was very happy working there. The work was interesting and the staff very nice. I soon got a place to stay and went back to Bandon every weekend calling at home when I could on my way back.

I sometimes met a man on my way to lunch, who would always say hello. One evening in September when I had been working in Bantry about three months I was up in my room intending to go to bed early when the woman I was lodging with came up and said her little boy wanted to go to Perks Amusement down the square and would I go with them for a short while. Perks were always well supported, they usually came every year. There was a bingo tent, the bumpers and stalls with lots of prizes among others. I bought a lot of tickets hoping to win a teddy bear for my little niece but had no luck, then somebody said hello, it was the man I often met at lunch time. He asked the woman I was staying with to introduce us and though I was already in a relationship things rested, as they say, and we married three years later.

Anniversary

Oh all the joy that ever was,
And all the hope that ere may be,
And all the laughter of the youth,
Are present in my love for thee.
And oh the joy of knowing you're there,
Makes light each burden, and each care.
The sighing wind and rushing sea,
Are present in my love for thee.
Though times may change and people too,
And Winter come and Summer go,
My love for you will never fade,
Just as in Springtime it will grow.
For hope and joy will never die,
They will both remain till time is done.
In hearts who feel the surge of love,
As when we two became as one.

Alone

I miss the times that used to be,
Those days that are no more.
I miss your thoughtful ways
As you helped with every chore.
I miss your careful painting
And papering just right,
I miss the love you gave to me,
I miss our chats at night.
I miss your step upon the stair,
With early morning tea.
I miss you, Oh! So very much,
I am no longer me.
One day we'll be together,
Won't than meeting be sublime!
We'll be happy ever after,
Not just once upon a time.

Shortly after we meeting he left his job in a hardware shop and came to the factory to work. We really enjoyed working there. When we got engaged the owner invited us to his house to celebrate and brought us gifts from Germany. We had just invested in a house in Bantry when the factory moved to Cobh, we got the option of going with it or to Germany where he had three other factories but decided to stay.

Before the factory moved to Cobh I got work in another local factory until that too closed! I then worked in a new hotel doing the accounts. It was always busy there as it was very popular and the staff very nice. I would have liked to stay working there but as I had a baby the hours were too long so I answered an advert for work as night telephonist in the local Post Office as the hours were more suitable. I was there for 12 years.

Both men and women were employed on the phones at night. It was always very busy in the summertime but in the winter we managed to have a tea break and took it in turns to bring some home cooking to have with it. The hours were eight to eleven or twelve or sometimes six to twelve and there was one man on all night. But as always time brings changes and eventually the telephone exchange went automatic. It was hard parting with the others and getting used to a different routine again.

For the previous four years my husband had worked as postman, but a few months after I finished work he was made redundant. After some months I went working in the office of Town & Country Homes and was there about a year when that too moved up the country. So I went to the office of a nearby garage where I worked for fifteen happy years. A little over two years before I finished work my brother had a bad accident, he was crushed by cattle at milking time, he survived for most of a year, his funeral was held at Bandon and I was surprised to see Peter who I had worked with so many years before waiting by the church gate, he did not say anything just hugged me and shook my hand, it meant so much to me that he had come, he had made such an effort not being well himself.

During my last year working they collected me and brought me home each day as the arthritis I had for a few years had got much worse. One sunny evening not long after I finished working I was sitting out in the garden when I saw a snail crawling along a mossy patch under the copper beech tree at the side of the house. I began to think of retirement and all the spare time I now had so I put together the following poem.

Retirement

I've had my day, it's come and gone,
And now with life I carry on.
No hours to watch nor time to keep,
The future lost in mystery deep.
But now there's time to look and see,
Natures wonders all for free.
I watched a snail go ambling by,
Its movements slow, the same as I.

Its little house was on its back,
Upon the moss, a silver track,
No rent to pay, nor ESB,
From all those overheads it's free.
The little birds that fly about,
You never hear them scream and shout.
Still happy though cold winters nigh,
Their song is always full of joy.
And then of course the busy bee,
All work no play, it's plain to see.
Happily flitting from hour to hour,
Gathering nectar from each flower.
The butterflies, the ladybirds,
The grasshoppers so gay,
All add their special little touch,
To everything in May.
Relaxed, no pressures now, that's me,
But at times I envy that busy bee.

Going back some years, when my eldest son started school he had a best friend called George, they are still friends today. George would come down through the fields to our house and John would take the same shortcut to his. On the way was the ruins of an old castle and one time passing there they saw a very neglected donkey. It had eaten what it could reach around it and was in very poor condition. It could hardly walk, its hooves were so bad. So they got it carrots and apples and fed it for a few days until we contacted the Donkey Sanctuary in Liscarrol. We then had to notify the local garda and one came to see it and of course no one admitted to owning it. Then the man from the sanctuary came and collected it. He said their vet would attend to it and it would be well looked after in the company of the other donkeys. The boys were very happy to have saved it. The following is a little poem I wrote about them at that time.

Space Boys

George and John to the moon have gone,
So we'll all have more peace on Earth.
They have gone away to the moon to stay,
To shine each night in the dark.
But the man in the moon will send them back soon,
And thank them for coming to stay,
As now he will know what peace really is,
Once they have gone away.
When our Space boys put their feet on the ground,
We hope they will keep them there,
And grow up strong knowing right from wrong,
Bringing happiness everywhere.
Then their friend on the moon will smile and say
He is glad to have met that pair,
And he'll think with joy of each little boy,
And the day they landed there.

I especially remember one evening when my two sons were doing their homework somehow their copybooks got mixed up and one got some stains on it, one accused the other and an argument started. Eventually after I removed the offending page peace was restored and as I sat down again by the fire I wrote the following poem.

My Copybook

When I was oh so very young,
My mother said to me,
'Now don't you blot your copybook',
She meant my soul, you see.

And if whilst going through life my son
On it you make a mess,
Be sure to rub it out again,
You only need confess.
Go to church each Sunday,
Receive Him all you can.
He will help you on life's way my boy,
He was the perfect man.
Keep Him in your sight always,
You will not go far astray,
You will find you have a friend in Him,
You can call on any day.

Now all this happened long ago,
And the road of life I've trod,
I have tried to keep as best I could,
My copybook for God.

Though sometimes I did make a mess,
And a blot came here and there,
I think I wiped the stains away,
With that little extra prayer.

When at times my feet would falter,
From His footsteps I would stray,
I'd call on Him to guide me -
He would and right away.
For His help is for the asking,
You will get courage in despair,
From a friend who never leaves you,
He is always waiting there.

I think I fell asleep last night,
While sitting on my chair,
I saw a shining roadway,
And a golden gateway there.
At this wondrous entrance,
There stood my lifelong friend,
He was waiting for me smiling,
A copybook in hand.
As I moved forward,
This copybook to see,
No blots or stains were on it,
It was shining bright, 'twas me.

Over the years the children had many pets, including goldfish, a hamster and a Budgie called Jamie one of them got at First Communion time. Once they had left for school I would usually listen to the radio for a while and have a cup of tea when I would talk to Jamie. I was surprised one morning when he answered me repeating what I was saying. He would follow us around the house and the neighbours children loved to hear him talking.

One August evening on our way back from a relatives funeral we called to my brother's farm. He was always interested in farming and to start had rented some piggery's from a local farmer. He would often tell how being up at their house one day, talking to the farmers wife, a gypsy woman came to the door. She had a baby in her arms. The farmer's wife told him to say the owners were not in. When he said that to her she said,

"They are in alright and they will lose a lot more than they would give me now."

 The following morning when they went to let the cattle out one was standing dead in the shed.

As well as farming my brother had some small dogs, Jack Russell's, Poms and Yorkies. When we went into the house that evening some puppies were in the kitchen, my daughter was in her element! My brother said she could have whichever one she wanted. On our way in there was a white puppy with a small head and very big ears sitting under the hall table. My brother said her breed was all kinds of everything and that a man who had bought some pigs from him a few days before must have brought it as it stayed sitting by his car, though he said it was not his. My daughter said she would take it as it might not get a home. So that is how Paddy joined our family and what a wonderful companion she turned out to be. On arriving home she had a bath and as we had a small dog basket and blanket we put it by the fire. She immediately went into it and went to sleep. The following day my daughter took her in her arms to town to get her a little walking harness. On her way home some man asked her, "Why are you taking the pig for a walk?" He was being smart but she did have that appearance. As she got older we were amazed at how knowing Paddy was, she treated us all differently and understood our different ways, if I left her out and her paws were wet coming in she would roll over for me to dry them, if my daughter left her out she would just run in. One son had a weakness for maltesers and so had Paddy. After a while not getting any she would beg, then she would give the odd whine until she got some. We felt she was like a caring Aunt in the family. In her own special way she welcomed them home from school and enjoyed playing ball with them. When they went to college the day they would be coming home on holidays I would tell her near the time they were due home, then she would wait at the door and I would hear her joyful bark when she saw them coming. Our neighbour next door would look after her if we were away for a day and take her for a while into her place. Once she gave Paddy some smarties, the next time she took her in Paddy went begging at the press, she remembered where the sweets were kept. My daughter had two pet mice (pip and squeak) she got for company in her flat. She brought them home during the holidays. One sunny day I put their cage on the coping near the grass outside the back door and said to Paddy, "Sit and mind them now.", not really expecting her to. She sat by the cage watching them. The cat next door that Paddy was friendly with came through the hedge, she ran through the grass and on seeing the mice came slowly towards the cage. Paddy growled at her and when she persisted hunted her through the hedge and came to sit by the cage again. Watching from the window I was so proud of her she made sure she kept them safe. After some years one of Paddy's paws seemed a bit tender to walk on. The Vet said it was probably her age and that she was a bit over weight. One of my sons got four little padded boots over the Internet for her and she managed to go for her walks much better wearing them. One morning in October 2000 I noticed Paddy was not her usual self but she seemed a bit better during the day. The following day she was not at all well so my son who was working near home at the time took her to the Vet who said he would keep her for the night in a special warm cage and to call in the morning. We phoned in the morning hoping she had improved and intending to drive out to see her but sadly she had died a little earlier. My other son and daughter came home. They made a coffin with her name and the date she died, putting in her toys and a bottle containing a letter telling about her and how much she meant to the family. The following is a poem in memory of her.

Paddy 1989-2000

Mans Best Friend

Four little paws that run to greet,
Two little eyes like pools so deep.
Your welcome bark and winning ways,
Can brighten up the darkest days.
Your love is great though you are small,
Good qualities you have them all.
You're there for me through thick and thin,
Regardless of what mood I'm in.
All that's good in friendship true,
Is wrapped up in little you.

After parting with Paddy I said that I would never have another dog. My daughter who was in France for a year or so got a present of a minature Yorkshire Terrier. On bringing him home she asked me to look after him. I soon got attached to Coco and I am very glad of his company now, not being able to get out very much. He sleeps in his little bed in my room and gives a great welcome to any visitors. This is a photo of him sitting by the fire, he likes his home comforts!

I realise and appreciate how lucky I am to have the company and help of my family and good neighbours, not everyone is as fortunate as they get older. Everyone wants to be useful and needed, sadly many feel isolated and alone. People still have much to give through their advice and wisdom learned from their many experiences. Grandchildren can benefit a lot from the love and attention of grandparents and older people. I wrote the following poem thinking of those who feel lonely and forgotten. It takes so little to brighten a person's day.

Tomorrow

Silence is golden so we are told,

But life can be lonely when you are old.

Maybe tomorrow someone will phone.

Maybe tomorrow I won't feel so alone.

Maybe tomorrow someone will call.

Maybe tomorrow a card in the hall.

Maybe tomorrow a knock on the door,

Maybe tomorrow a friend like before.

Maybe tomorrow with an hour to spare,

Maybe tomorrow someone on that chair.

Maybe tomorrow my thoughts I can share,

Maybe tomorrow someone will care.

Like many others throughout the world Padre Pio is my favourite saint. He has helped me many times especially in a wonderful way many years ago. My Aunt, who I had gone to live with as a child, when I got married always came to us for Christmas and would usually stay for a few months. The February after her last Christmas with us she got very ill and lived only a few days. But for Padre Pio's help I would not have kept going. I talked to him. My children at that time were aged seven, five and three years so I needed to be able to look after them. About six weeks after my Aunt died my five year old son was playing outside with others in some sand drawing lines with stones. His stone he had got from a nearby ditch. One little girl said to him, "That stone looks like a monk." Having heard me talk about Padre Pio he then ran home with it and said, "Mam, I have a stone that looks like a monk, I'll leave it here on the table." I was upstairs at the time and when I came down and saw it I immediately felt Padre Pio was very near and helping me. From then on I was able to cope. There was a mission some time later and I got it blessed. I have it always. This is a picture of it here. I read a lot about Padre Pio and the miracles he has worked. One about a little blind girl who's

Gran was always praying to him to make her see. He called her to the altar as they attended his mass and said prayers over her and for the first time, much to the delight of her Gran, she could see though there were no pupils in her eyes. Another miracle I thought was wonderful, a woman went to confession to Padre Pio during which she said to him doctors had told her she could never have children. He answered her and said,

"Bring him to me and I will christen him."

Within a year she came with the baby to Padre Pio and he became the priest who assisted Padre Pio at his last mass.

This is a poem I wrote about Padre Pio which was published by *The Voice of Padre Pio* in Italy.

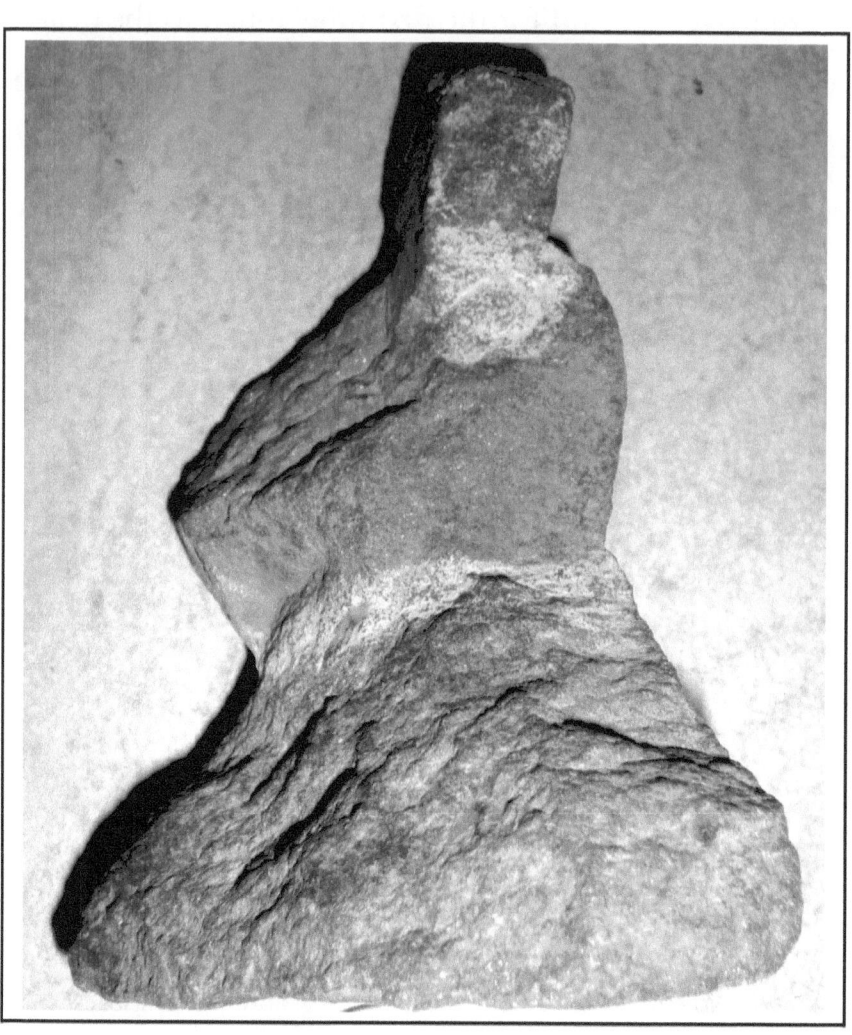

Padre Pio

Padre Pio, this man of God,
He walked the path that Jesus trod.
A life of prayer and years of pain,
He cured and blessed in Jesus' name.
From many lands they came to see,
He who bore the marks of Calvary.
This holy Friar a simple prayer
That's from the heart will always hear,
And answer in a wondrous way.
So talk to him, and simply pray.

I would like to share with you a poem about a grotto a few miles from where I now live. It was put there by a priest near his old homestead in memory of his parents.

Our Lady of Trawlebawn

There's a Grotto near the roadside,
In a place called Trawlebawn.
Do not pass it in your hurry,
Spare a moment for to pray.
You will find you can cope better,
With the pressures of your day.
In that luxury of silence,
You will find another way.
Any worries will seem lighter,
And your frustrations cease.
Amid the rugged rocks and heather,
She will give to you Her peace.
The peace that comes from Heaven,
That the world does not know,
As you continue on your journey,
Will be with you as you go.

The passing of time always brings with it many happy events including the arrival of grandchildren, they bring so much joy to the grandparents who look forward to seeing them, as many have more time now to enjoy them than they had when rearing their own children. The following is a poem I wrote to remember this much looked forward to wonderful occasion.

The New Arrival

Ten little fingers and copycat toes,
A bonny round face and wee button nose,
That would describe me a little, you see,
But I can assure you there is much more to me.

I cry when I'm hungry and make quite a noise
And I'll soon fill your house with my laughter and
toys,
I can wind you around my wee finger, you see,
As I smile at the angels that watch over me.

I need your guidance to know right from wrong,
So I can grow up with a character strong.
I know when you check me it's because you care,
And nothing will sever the love that we share.
Now I will finish by saying I'm so glad,
That God chose you to be my Mom and Dad.

So dear reader, thank you for coming down memory lane with me and I hope you enjoyed it a much as I did looking back.

My wish is that you too will have many good times to think back on and that you will always make today tomorrow's happy memories.

An Irish Farewell

May the good Lord bless and keep you,
Till we meet again someday.
May you always walk in His light,
And in His friendship stay.

May your days be ever happy
And your friendships all prove true.
May the good Lord bless and keep you,
Is my parting wish to you.

May you know the poor when you have got
More than your needed share.
May you help the old and lonely,
And keep them from despair.

May you store in life the treasures,
That no rust can e'er destroy,
The ones you can take with you,
When you bid this world goodbye.

That your cross in life you'll carry,
With a will that you may share
In the one He bore for us,
In that love beyond compare.

That your road through life may leave behind
A trail of good deeds done,
And the Angels fly to meet you,
When your journey here is done.

That's my prayerful wish from Ireland
And if to it you are true,
'Twill ensure old friends will meet again,
Where all good wishes come true.

Acknowledgements

My heartfelt thanks to Jesus, Mary and Padre Pio for their constant help and being always there for me.

To my family for their kindness and encouragement.

Picture Credits:

p10 Celtic Cross by Bitter like a Coffee @ Flickr.com

p13 Christmas Window by Stuart Richards

p22 Thistle with Bee by John Haslam

p26 Robin by Chapmankj75 @ Flickr.com

p36 Shamrock by Jonathan Philips

p44 Spring Bee by Lida Rose

p48 Summer by Cornelia Kopp

p48 Red Squirrel by Giles Gonthier

p52 Winter Meal by Jan Tik

p58 Mother&Child by John Barreiros

p64 Two Swans by Subramanain Kablan

p66 Lone Swan by Lionel Grove

p72 Snails by Hannah S Metana

p76 Full Moon by Luz A. Villa

p92 Alone by H. Kopp Delaney